Channel of Love

Channel of Love

A Story of Healing through Divine Love,
A Love that Never Fails and Never Dies

Susan Carroll

ISBN: Hardcover 978-1-9845-7829-7
Softcover 978-1-9845-7833-4
eBook 978-1-9845-7828-0

Print information available on the last page.

Rev. date: 05/14/2020

To order additional copies of this book, contact:
Xlibris
1-888-795-4274
www.Xlibris.com
Orders@Xlibris.com
803611

To my spirit, who has waited patiently and lovingly all these years for our voice to be heard, for our story to be told.

Contents

Preface

This story is the record of my encounter with divine love. It took place at a time in my life when nothing else but the love of God could see me through the darkness of alcoholism and depression. I always knew that, one day, I would write and publish this book, but it took nine years for me to find the courage to do so. I knew God wanted me to speak my truth and tell the story of my miraculous redemption and transformation. I understand that, for many readers, it will be an unbelievable story, one that simply could not have taken place and was, therefore, contrived and created in an unstable mind and spirit. For how can there be such a direct communion with God, guides, and departed loved ones?

I know what I have experienced and have recorded the events from memory and journals to the best of my ability. During the writing process, I also allowed my spirit to come forward and bring inspiration to the writing process, helping to choose words or remember important pieces of the story that I may have forgotten or failed to record. At times, my heart felt as if my spirit was telling the story and I was merely the scribe. What joyful writing that was!

In present time, I still receive written messages of love and support from my guides in heaven who love and watch over me, but I have no direct communication with God, Mother God, Erob, or my mother. I know in my heart that they are continuing to send their love, support and guidance, but in a different way now. When I pray for guidance or just sit quietly and listen with my heart, I hear the same message, "Go with love. Always choose love."

The completion of this book is an assignment long overdue, but it's never too late to speak the truth. As my spirit told me many years ago, "You will tell the story and the truth shall set you free." I am now, indeed, free. Thank you to all who have loved me, guided me, inspired me to tell this story of never ending love that has no boundaries and no end. Love never fails. Love wins.

March 9, 2020 Susan Carroll

Chapter One

The Beginning

When we least expect it, a shift happens. We often do not see or feel it coming, but it is there, silently waiting to be recognized as the hand of God beginning to move in our lives. Once in place, this force is so powerful that it can rearrange an entire life in an instant and remain in place forever.

Before the shift, my life, spanning five decades, was just a story. When I was a child, I felt as if the story was being written for me by some invisible, all-powerful force that was responsible for writing all children's life stories. I saw that some children had better stories than others, stories that were full of love and joy and secure in ways that I could only witness but never experience. In my innocent mind, I did not understand why I was given this story, but I intuitively knew that it was mine, my part to play as best I could. The seeds of insecurity, fear, anxiety, and the longing for unconditional love were all planted during this time and flourished well during my teenage and adult years.

My mother and father, as all parents do, did the best they knew how to create a safe and loving home for their children. In some ways, they were successful, but in other ways, they were not. Working as a physician, my father was able to provide a financially stable home, but together, they struggled to create a home that was emotionally stable and secure for their four children. My earliest memories of my life with my parents, my brothers, and my sister are filled with both great joy and great pain. Love and joy could be present one moment and then gone in an instant only to be replaced with anger, fear, or uncertainty.

In my story, my mother struggled with depression, as well as alcoholism. My father was much more stable, but due to his work schedule, he was often an absent character in my daily life. My mother's struggles continued throughout my childhood and beyond. I have always had great compassion for her life story, even as it spilled pain into mine. When she was a young child, both her mother and father passed away. Tuberculosis and pneumonia stole the lives of her parents and left her abandoned in grief. Even though loving relatives adopted her and cared for her, this grief was with her always. She was unable to lay it down, so she learned to carry it with her, hidden from sight, but always present in her heart. Grief would silently direct the acts of her story. I believe that she never recovered from this loss of primary love. When her own children were born, she loved them fiercely but was never able to emotionally connect with or express her love freely. I know that she loved us deeply, but there were no hugs, kisses, or declarations of love in our home. Her disconnect was too great, a valley of grief that we, as her children, could not cross.

From outward appearances, my mother seemed to be a successful mother and wife. Behind the scenes was another story. She played her role well but was all the while disconnected from the love she so desperately wanted and needed. When depression and anxiety consumed her mind, she consumed alcohol. It was the numbing potion that took the pain and tucked it away at least for a few hours. For her, it became a nightly ritual (much to my father's disapproval) to reward herself with a drink or several before my father arrived home from work. Looking back, I now believe that her depression was so great that she was merely enduring each day, accomplishing her duties as wife and mother so that she could then allow herself to drink at night. Her goal was to become comfortably numb. As the years passed and as she continued to drink more and more, raging alcoholism took hold of her mind, body, and spirit and refused to let go. In the end, it had its way with her.

I learned as a young child that, in order to receive love from my mother, I needed to bring love. I also learned my love was not always accepted, much less returned. Instinctively, I knew there was an invisible wall between us and that this wall could not be crossed over except during certain times and only if permission was given. I did not really understand the rules of this game we were playing, and it made me sad each time I lost. I loved my mother unconditionally and, in my child's heart, forgave her every time I did not receive a hug or kiss when I longed for one. I forgave her every time I witnessed her reach for a drink instead of love.

Since my job was to make the best of the story I had been given, instead of complaining, I always tried to be a good and helpful little girl. This was how I earned love and attention. If I cleaned my room without being asked (maybe my brother's too), my mother would always smile and be happy for a while. If she was happy, then she would not want to drink, and all would be well. These were my gifts to my mother. This was how I learned to exchange love with my mother. I relished what love was returned to me no matter how small or fleeting. For those moments in time, love was mine. I was joyful because I had been rewarded for being a good girl. I had successfully earned my mother's love. I had played the game well, and I had won.

As my story continued, I carried this strategy into my adolescent years and continued to make it work for me. It was the 1970s, and I began to create a new reality for my spirit through school, friends, and activities. I was growing into a beautiful young woman, and it was my time to shine. I began to distance myself from my mother's painful, depressing world. I discovered how powerful the love of a boyfriend, or even just a close friend, could be. I also discovered that a driver's license and permission to use a car equaled freedom! What a joy that was to have the power to release myself from pain and move towards love! I could fly away towards joy and love, and my ticket was earned by pleasing my parents.

In the 1970s, it was all about the freedom to choose whatever brought joy, peace, and love. I totally embraced the spirit of that era. It felt good to be carried on that wave of unconditional love and acceptance. I indulged myself in it all—the music, the fashion, the spirit of complete freedom to choose and create what I desired. I also indulged in experimenting with alcohol and drugs, which was the norm in my social group. Private parties and school-sponsored events, such as dances and games, always included alcohol and marijuana. The consumption usually took place in a parked car at the location of the event. Any adult supervision (usually teachers) appeared to turn a blind eye to it all. Perhaps they did not care or, who knows, maybe they were indulging as well. The legal drinking age was eighteen, and if you could not find someone to purchase it for you, beer and wine could be easily purchased with a false ID. Marijuana could be found without much effort just by walking to the nearest parking lot. There was always someone waiting to share the high. No police or resource officers were present. We, as free spirits, were in control, and it was all such an easy game to play.

When I entered high school and was introduced to marijuana, I discovered that this substance had the power to give me the peace and calm that I had never before experienced. It had the power to erase any feelings of anxiety and uncertainty that hovered in my mind. When I smoked marijuana, my world was a happy place. Alcohol made me feel even better. I also began to smoke cigarettes during this time because my first boyfriend smoked. If time permitted between classes, we would meet for a cigarette break. In order to keep the smokers out of the bathrooms, my school provided a designated smoking area behind the main building. It was here that my boyfriend and I came together to feed our nicotine addictions.

During my junior and senior years of high school, I chased the high on the weekends and managed to be a fairly decent student during the week. Looking back, I believe that my parents were aware of the drinking but chose not to confront me. At that time, in the seventies, the attitude of many parents was, "We don't approve of drinking, but it's better than doing drugs. Please stay away from the drugs because they are dangerous. They will destroy your life."

This was a dangerous compromise and, for me, would have long-lasting consequences. By the time

I graduated, I was drinking almost every weekend. I could not wait to get to college where, away from my parents, my choices would all be under my control. I would be free to feed my growing indulgence for alcohol. I would be free to smoke anytime I pleased. The seeds of addiction had been planted and were waiting eagerly to be watered.

And so the water began to flow.

Chapter Two

Freedom and Beyond

The four-year college I chose to attend did indeed allow me to water my growing addictions. In fact, it allowed me to saturate them. The year was 1975, and the drinking age for beer and wine was still eighteen. My parents, like many other parents, believed their daughter was safely tucked away for the next four years to study and earn a degree. Surely, I would not be allowed to indulge in any dangerous or immoral behavior.

I was pleasantly surprised to find that, even in this very traditional all women's college, the regulations and attitudes toward drinking were very liberal. The dorm mothers that were placed in all freshman dorms served as sentinels to prevent any male visitors from entering past the reception rooms. While the school took a stand on preventing sexual encounters, it took no stand on drinking. Both alcohol and smoking were allowed in all of the dorms. Everyone drank, and the majority of students smoked. Alcohol was present in all school-sponsored events. It wasn't a dance or a party without a keg of beer or some punch made from whatever liquor and wine were available. At these events, alcohol consumption and drinking to excess was the norm, not the exception. On the other hand, illegal drugs were not allowed. Possession of any drugs would result in automatic expulsion.

During the next four years, I continued the pattern of excessive drinking. I indulged primarily on the weekends so that there was time and a clear mind to focus on my classes during the week. There was too much at stake to do otherwise. I knew that, if my grades started to fall and I had to leave college, my world that I had so carefully crafted would come tumbling down. If I was forced to return home, my freedom and my ability to water my seeds would be taken from me. I was determined that, no matter what, that tumbling down was never going to happen. I would do whatever was necessary to protect my world. I would play the game according to their rules. So a few months into my freshman year, I made the decision to give up marijuana. As I released this drug from my life, I began to fully embrace my love of drinking and smoking.

As this love affair began to flourish, alcohol and cigarettes became my best friends. They were always by my side, ready to soothe the anxieties and stress that were common for me during those years. They became my reward for a job well done and my solace when things did not go well. They brought peace to my mind and body. By the time I graduated from college in 1979, I had earned a degree in psychology and special education. I had also secured my path to alcoholism. As I began to search for a secure place in the world, I carried my best friends with me into my future.

After college, I secured a teaching position in special education. I was barely earning enough to support myself, but I never went hungry, nor did I ever go without alcohol or cigarettes. I continued to chase the high on the weekends, but never let it interfere with my teaching responsibilities. I began to master the art of being a functional alcoholic but was in complete denial of the truth about my life.

In 1985, I met my husband, and a year later, we were married. In this new phase of my life, I continued to balance my drinking and my responsibilities. I focused on creating a life that allowed me to drink and still function as a fairly responsible wife, mother, and professional. The only time I stopped drinking completely was during my two pregnancies in 1990 and 1994. My sons were born four years apart. Once the pregnancy and nursing were finished, I began to drink again.

My children were, and continue to be, my greatest blessing. They were each one a gift from God. They inspired me to focus less on my addictions and more on the love that had been given to me through the grace of God. There were, however, some nagging questions that often entered my mind, "Was God still loving me when I chose to continue to drink after having been given such precious gifts? How was that possible?" In my way of thinking, all love was earned by being good. The concept of unconditional love and grace did not apply to me. Even though I did carry some shame for drinking and smoking, I convinced myself that I was still a good mother in every other way. My husband and I were creating a loving family. Surely, God saw that much was true.

In the years that followed the birth of my youngest son, I began to honestly consider the possibility that I had entered into the world of serious alcoholism and genuine addiction. If my husband was worried or suspected the same, he kept his feelings to himself. My husband had always been very tolerant of my drinking habit. This was true for two reasons: one, he enjoyed drinking as well and participated in what had become the nightly ritual; two, he was never confrontational with me. He gave me the freedom to make my own choices and decisions about my life and did not try to control me in any way. This was one of the reasons I loved him and chose to marry him. Tragically, fifteen years later, it was he, not I, who suffered the mental and physical effects of alcohol abuse. After living for many years with severe depression and chronic alcoholism and choosing not to seek treatment, he passed away from liver disease. At the time of his passing, we had been married for almost thirty years.

When my sons began elementary school, I made the decision to return to teaching full time. When they were young, I had taken time off to be at home with them instead of choosing to work and place them in daycare. I returned to the pattern of chasing the high on the weekends but never during the week. I took my teaching responsibilities seriously and wanted to be my best in the classroom.

When I look back at my life during this time, I see beauty, love, joy, and many blessings. I had an incredible family, a good marriage, two beautiful children, and a meaningful job. When I indulged in drinking, I was not drinking to numb unpleasant feelings or to escape the pain. I was drinking to feel good and to chase the high. Little did I know that this joyful life of mine was about to take an unexpected turn in a direction I did not know was possible. A shift was coming, ready to take me to a place where darkness and despair were waiting for my arrival. Act 2 of my life was set to begin. With or without my permission, it was coming.

And so it came.

CHAPTER THREE

SLIPPING INTO DARKNESS

In 2008, my mother passed away, and my world began to crumble. The dismantling of my life had begun. I did not know it yet, but during the next seven years, I would bury my father and my husband as well. My world, as I had known it, would never be the same.

At the age of seventy-five, my mother suffered a massive stroke. She was placed in an excellent, highly reputable rehabilitation facility with the hopes that she could regain some of the abilities she had lost. The brain damage was extensive. She had lost all language, leaving her unable to communicate. She was unable to speak, read, or write. The only word that was uttered from her lips was, "Why?" In her attempts to communicate, she would repeat this one word over and over, believing that she was speaking a sentence or asking a question. "Why, why, why, why" was all we heard while, in her mind, she believed that she was speaking words into a sentence. She also lost the use of the right side of her body. She was unable to move her right arm and leg. Unable to walk, she was now bound to a wheelchair. In an instant, my mother's life had been dismantled.

As the days and weeks passed and reality set in, her frustration and sorrow swelled. Depression and anger came to be her constant companion. She was losing her will to live. After little success in the rehabilitation facility, our family was told that because she had shown no real progress and appeared to have no motivation due to depression, it was time for her to go. Where was she to go? Considering her extensive medical needs, none of us felt secure in our ability to care for her in our home. The staff at the rehabilitation facility advised us to search for a long-term placement that could meet her needs. With little time and no direction, my family made the decision to transfer her to a nursing facility in the city where my brother lived.

My brother and I began the journey of caring for our mother, as she moved into the next phase of her life. We shared the responsibility of overseeing her care, as well as offering her our love and support. We alternated weekend visits and both of us communicated with nurses and staff during the week. My mother was unable to speak on the phone, so we relied heavily on the staff to report her daily mental and physical condition. This attempt at long-distance caregiving caused great anxiety for me. When I knew or suspected that she was suffering mentally or physically, I wanted nothing more than to be by her side and be the voice that would bring her comfort and relief from pain. Since I was unable to make the two-and-a-half-hour drive during the week, I depended on my brother to bring comfort to her. If my brother was not available or not willing to go, I was forced to sit with my anxiety and guilt of not being there for my mother.

As time passed, I learned through experience that I could not rely on the accuracy of the many different staff reports I received by phone. Nor could I trust that she was receiving the care that she needed. As my anxiety continued to increase, so did my drinking. I drank to push down the feelings of helplessness that were rising within me. It all felt so out of control, and there was nothing I could do to make it better. For the first time in my life, I began to drink to forget.

My brother, struggling with his own emotions about caring for our mother, began to disconnect and distance himself. He would still show for scheduled visits, but if there were problems and she was upset and angry or frustrated about not being able to communicate what was wrong, he would end the visit and exit the nursing home. As much as he loved her, he could not, or chose not, to be present in her suffering. We never discussed it, but I believe he felt totally helpless over this situation that was spiraling out of his control.

During the first year that my mother lived at the nursing home, I continued to teach full time, as well as care for my husband and two teenage sons. I was continually exhausted, stressed, and confused about the best way to handle it all. When my schedule allowed, I drank. I began to rely on alcohol to numb out the constant stress that was present in my daily life. Drinking was no longer fun. It had become a necessary evil. Alcohol and cigarettes became my tranquilizers. I had no worries about where this dependency might lead because I did not care. I had shifted into survival mode. I convinced myself that I was justified in doing whatever was necessary in order to avoid a meltdown while continuing to put one foot in front of the other.

Something had to give, so in 2006, as my mother began her second year at the nursing facility, I made the decision to resign from my teaching position. I made this decision so that I would be available for her care, but I also felt I had no other choice. I had proven that I could not handle all that life was presenting to me. I could not balance long-distance caregiving with full-time work along with my family responsibilities. My husband and I made the decision to move my mother out of the nursing facility and into our home. We began to make plans to build a handicapped-accessible addition to our home that would accommodate her needs. My husband was a builder, so we would be able to build at a reduced rate with only the cost of materials as an expense. The plan was in place, and now, all we needed to do was follow it. Helpless anxiety was being replaced by newly found hope and a fierce determination to see our plan through. My husband and I worked to complete the additional space as quickly as our schedules and finances would allow.

During the next year, as we continued to work our plan, I continued to care for my mother long distance as best I could. She was beginning to show signs of physical and mental degeneration. Long hours of sitting in a wheelchair combined with the effects of the stroke resulted in circulatory problems. She began to suffer massive leg cramps that could not be controlled with medication. They could strike at any time, and she would have to endure the powerful pain of contraction until her muscles decided to let go and relax. She also began to have blood clots in her legs that resulted in many hospitalizations. My mother experienced constant anxiety over what was happening to her body. Her fear of the pain that could come at any time and her inability to speak and say what was wrong produced tremendous anger and agitation. She began to rage on a daily basis and was now seen by the staff as a resident with a behavior problem. This was the last thing we needed to happen. It was not part of our plan. When she wasn't raging, she was depressed. I kept reminding her and myself that, as soon as the addition to our home was finished, she would be moved, and everything would be better. I had to believe that. It was our only hope.

We had a plan, but life had other plans. As we neared the end of construction in January of 2008, my mother had a series of falls as she was being transferred from her bed to her wheelchair. One of these falls resulted in a broken hip that went undiagnosed for days. Another fall resulted in a head injury. Both required hospital visits. For the next few weeks, she rotated in and out of the hospital due to poor vitals. Her physical and mental condition was beginning to deteriorate. I realized that our opportunity to move her had passed. God was closing that door. I understood that, if I tried to move her at this point, I would not be able to care for her medical needs by myself in my home. At best, I could move her to a hospital in my city, but what would be the point in that?

There was reality staring me in the face. I had been defeated. I had failed. I was sad but mostly angry. Angry at whom? Who was responsible for this nightmare? Should I be angry at myself for not insisting that she be moved earlier, even if that meant moving her to another nursing facility in my city? Should I be angry at my husband for not making sure that the addition was finished earlier, even if that meant he had to sacrifice his work responsibilities and finances? Should I be angry at the nursing home staff who were negligent with my mother? Or perhaps I should be angry at God for not protecting my mother just a little bit longer until we could get her moved? Isn't God supposed to ensure our plans when they are made with a loving heart and pure intentions? I blamed all of the above and more. My anger began to override the intense pain I was feeling, and I carried it along with my broken heart to the bitter end.

During the next couple of weeks, as my mother continued to rotate in and out of the hospital, I was with her as much as possible. I experienced so many emotions and drank to erase the ones I could not bear to feel and carry in my heart. I began to pray for her release from the suffering. Even though I was not ready to let her go, I wanted the suffering to end. I had failed in my attempt to control it all. Now there was nothing else to do but turn her over to God and wait for whatever was coming. In many ways, it felt as if her death would be a relief. To this day, I have no idea if my mother felt the same and if she realized that her life was coming to an end.

My mother entered the hospital for the final time on April 1, 2008. She was admitted for clots in her leg. A clot of blood traveling to her lung and then onward to her heart would be what delivered the final blow. The last time I saw my mother conscious, she was angry and upset about something she wanted to say to me but could not communicate. She would yell and scream (was she in pain?) and then rest for a few minutes only to begin again a few minutes later. This continued for several hours. During a calm moment, I told her that I needed to leave for a little while. The truth was that I could not take it anymore. I needed a break, or else I was going to end up on the floor in a puddle of tears. I did not want her to witness that on top of her growing distress. So, I kissed her good-bye and left. Halfway down the hall, I heard her yelling out again. I stopped and paused for a moment, unsure of what to do. Was she calling out for me to come back? In the next moment, my feet were moving forward, as if they had a will of their own. As I exited the building, I could feel a wave of tears swelling up to be released. I walked quickly to my car and slid behind the wheel. Then through an explosion of tears and sobs, I yelled out to God, "It's too much! Make it stop!" I do not remember how long I sat there in that seat, crying and yelling those words out to God, but I do remember my hands were gripping the steering wheel with a tremendous force, as my forehead was pressed against it. In this position, as my body rocked back and forth, I began to release some of the rage, fear, and grief that I had been carrying for years. This was beyond a desperate prayer. I had crossed the line into demanding that God take action. I felt I could not survive anymore. When my mind and body were spent and my heart said "enough", I dried my eyes and drove out of the parking lot and away from my mother's hospital room.

I chose not to return to my mother that evening. I received no calls reporting her progress, nor did I make any calls asking for information. Instead, I spent time alone, restoring my strength and preparing myself for whatever the next day would bring. I had no feeling that she might take a turn in a different direction. She had been distressed and anxious, but that was to be expected. She had seemed fully alive and, other than the clots in her leg, was in no serious danger physically. Little did I know that, sometime during the night, my mother and God would take control of everything. A major shift was happening, and once the process began, it would change everything. That evening, my mother began her exit from this world. Blood clots that had been resting in her leg dislodged and traveled to rest in her lung.

When I returned to my mother the next morning, she appeared to be sleeping. An hour later, when she did not wake up, the medical staff determined she was in a coma and predicted that the clots would continue to grow and travel until they reached her heart. I was told by her doctors there was nothing else to be done.

Only my mother and God know what happened during the night, as she lay alone in her hospital bed. Perhaps they reached an understanding of what was going to happen. Or maybe somehow she understood my despair and lack of strength to carry on and made the decision to let go of this life. Is that why she was calling me back? To say, "No more"? To say, "Goodbye"? When her body began the process of shutting down and her spirit was preparing to leave, I found myself at a loss for words. There was nothing left to say except "I love you," so these were the words I spoke to her. In my heart, I knew she heard me, and in her heart, she sent her love back to me.

Her death was not an easy one. Her body struggled to let go. I remained by her side for hours until my brothers arrived. I could watch no more of this brutal process. This was not how I wanted to remember my mother. With the excuse of needing money and clean clothes, I left and returned home. The truth was I needed to escape and numb myself with alcohol. I needed to erase the memory of what I had witnessed. Around midnight that evening, my brother called to say that it was over. She had passed. Through the haze of alcohol, I remember crying myself to sleep. I returned the next morning to begin the process of funeral arrangements. I also began the process of carrying the guilt of not being strong enough to stay by her side through it all. I felt as if I had failed her in so many ways, and if this were true, then no amount of guilt would be too great for me to carry.

This was the end of her life story and the beginning of the next chapter of mine. Beyond the relief that her suffering was over and beyond the grief of saying good-bye, I was aware of another emotion that was present, and it made me uneasy. I could feel the darkness lurking, waiting patiently for me to acknowledge its presence. When I did, it was ready to descend and begin its walk with me.

And so we walked.

Chapter Four

Walking in Darkness

The months that followed my mother's death were dark and blurry. I could not see clearly. I was forced to find my way through the darkness alone. No one offered to come alongside me and be my companion. I blamed myself and others for her death. I was no longer teaching and had too much time to focus on all that had happened. My thoughts focused like a laser, always pointing to the pain and anger, which I then must carry. I saw no way to put it down and, therefore, no release.

If only I had been able to make better choices or take different actions. If only others had done what they were supposed to do, maybe this story would have had a happier ending. Early on, I realized that my anger needed to have targets. Surely, I alone was not responsible for the series of events that led to my mother's death. Who else could I bring along with me on this walk through the darkness?

My husband, who should have done more, was my first target. He became a silent witness to my walk, refusing to join me and yet watching and listening to it all. He was silent when I suggested that his lack of speed in constructing the home addition might have been intentional because, perhaps, he never really wanted my mother to come. His silence only served to fuel my anger. How can you forgive someone who refuses to admit any wrongdoing? He never disagreed when I said, "We could have moved her sooner. If you had wanted to, we could have gotten her out of the facility." For my husband, regret and sorrow and, maybe, forgiveness never got the chance to come forth. Dead silence stood in its way and said, "We are not going there."

As time passed, my anger, having no release, continued to grow and become a powerful force. It left my silent husband and began to move toward God. The monologue went something like this, "How could you let it end this way? I would have never left her alone in her hospital room had I known what was coming. Did I not deserve to receive a nudge to stay with her? Where were you when she fell over and over and suffered such painful injuries? She had no voice to speak for herself, so why were you not protecting her when she could not protect herself? Please tell me what was the point of all this suffering?" Once again, I heard no answers, only dead silence. I had no choice but to take the anger back and let it sit with me where it now seemed to belong. I told myself, if only I had been stronger, braver, more faithful, and loving, God would not have let it end this way.

This grief, shame, and anger would follow me into the next chapter of my story, setting the stage for what was to come. I had allowed myself to sink into a depression where I stayed for many months. My spirit was not allowed in this newly created space of despair. Grief, shame, and anger were allowed to enter but only to be numbed by a steady flow of alcohol. They were my unwanted but necessary companions. I no longer cared about anything other than myself and the painful state in which I now existed. My mental and physical health did not concern me. I convinced myself that my husband and my sons could take care of themselves.

My mother passed away in April. By July, my oldest son was preparing to move to begin his first year of college. After my son left, the sorrow I had been carrying intensified. I was being forced to let go of love again. I mourned the death of my mother, and I mourned the loss of my oldest child all at the same time. I tried to push myself into the letting-go process that I understood I had to complete. I had no choice because life was not going to give me a break on this lesson. I was not a ready and willing student. I did not feel brave. I did not feel confident that I could survive, much less master this experience of letting go. I felt myself sinking further down into a wave of sorrow and despair.

As I readied myself to ride this wave of unending sorrow, I looked to alcohol to be my constant companion. If I had to endure this experience, then I would do so feeling as little as possible. In other words, I would numb out, somehow get through the worst of it, and then try to move on.

After my son left, I chose to move into the additional space we had built for my mother. The construction was finished. The space was beautiful. It was ready and waiting for someone to move in and enjoy. It contained a small kitchen and living area with a bedroom and a handicapped bathroom. There was even a small porch out back with a beautiful view of the trees, flowers, and field beyond. It was the peaceful, safe place that I dreamed of for my mother. The perfect place for her to live out what remained of her life. It was also the perfect space for me to isolate myself and attempt to drink away my anger and despair.

Looking back, I see that my husband allowed me to do this, not because he approved, but because he felt helpless to stop what was coming. He was afraid of and powerless against such despair and anger. I do not remember any discussion about my drinking and isolation. He simply said nothing. Since my youngest son was consumed with his high school activities, he had little time to focus on what was going on with me. I feel sure he had some sense of my depression and alcohol abuse, but he also felt powerless to change anything. It was best to steer clear of Mom. To this day, I have no idea what was discussed between the two of them concerning my behavior. Shame prevents me from having that conversation with my son.

I cannot say how long I chose to stay in what-would-have-been my mom's space because I do not remember. I had hit a dead end, and I knew I was going nowhere. I saw no clear path in front of me, but I knew I had reached a fork in the road. Do I bear right or left? I had no clear vision. No light was with me, illuminating the correct path. Either way, I could not see what was waiting for me. In the midst of my confusion, my survival instincts were alive and well despite the fact that my mind and body were drowning in alcohol. The voice was not loud or strong, but I heard it clearly, saying, "Move towards love. Move towards love and whatever else is waiting for you there." Looking back, I believe this moment was a ray of grace and clear vision flowing together as one. It was a gift from God flowing into my spirit. My spirit was saying to me, "There is still love here. Look around you. What do you see?" I listened to that voice, and I stopped drinking long enough to take a long hard look. What I saw was my family, who was still loving me unconditionally. What I felt was my love for them. I asked myself an important question, "Where are you going with this?" The answer

I heard back was, “Nowhere. There’s nowhere for you to go with this except back to your family, back to your life, back to love.”

From that moment on, I began to try to pull myself back together. As I did, I somehow managed to bring my reality into focus. My vision was returning, and I could see that my life lay in pieces before me, but I did not know how to place those broken pieces back together correctly. I knew that I needed help and guidance, and I also knew that the help I needed would be beyond what my family could give me. Since I was still angry with God, praying for divine guidance seemed foolish. Besides, I wasn’t ready to let go of that anger just yet. God, I’m sure, was well aware of that fact.

A few weeks later, I began to see a therapist, who specialized in recovery from trauma. His office was located in the same building as my health club membership. Over the years, as I was passing by his office door on my way to the weight room or pool, I often wondered about the people who went through those doors and the problems that led them there. I even expressed silent gratitude that I was not one of them. Life had been kinder to me.

I chose not to share my life of addiction with this compassionate, kind man. I was not ready to let go. I convinced myself that my alcoholism was not the cause of my emotional problems, and since it was not the cause, it deserved no attention. The trauma was what was holding me back. I believed that, through this specialized therapy, all the trauma in my mind, body, and spirit could be released. I would purge myself of all the grief, despair, rage, and guilt that I was still carrying from the experience of witnessing my mother's downward spiral and death. This was my simple plan, and I convinced myself that it would work.

What prevented me from being honest about my drinking? Was it shame? Was I afraid that I would be forced to stop completely if I was not ready to do so? An honest answer would be, maybe a little of both. Since this therapist had no knowledge of my alcoholism, he focused all my treatment sessions on resolving grief and trauma. Unknown to him, every evening, I was drowning my grief in alcohol and pacifying my anxieties with cigarettes. After months of therapy specifically designed for releasing traumatic memories, I saw and felt no real progress. The haunting memories continued to cause me emotional stress. My mind, body, and spirit were not giving anything up. I made the decision to stop therapy.

I continued to drink daily, but the amount I drank was less. Day after day, I was putting one foot in front of the other, walking through days that felt as if they had no real purpose.

Some part of me must have believed that recovery was possible, that time would heal all wounds. So with no other options, my spirit kept marching forward. Little did I know that with this march step by step, I was preparing to meet God. A perfect divine love, full of redemptive power was waiting for me down my path, and all I had to do was keep walking.

"Just keep taking the next step," my spirit said. And so I did. Redemption, restoration, and hope for the future—I would learn all these things were possible.

And so much more.

Chapter Five

A Way Opens

In a space that was far beyond the reality in which I lived, my story continued to unfold. The gifts of redemption, healing grace, and unconditional love began to rain down on me. These gifts that God so mercifully gave to me were the beginning of my healing journey, a journey that continues to this day.

I was raised to seek the spirit of Christ in church. Growing up, I attended an Episcopal church in a small, conservative Southern town. As a child, I believed God lived in that beautiful church, and if you wanted to talk or spend time with him, you had to enter that building. Christmas, Easter, and Sunday mornings, he was there waiting for me to show up. At the age of thirteen, I was confirmed in this church, passing all oral and written tests on the doctrine of the church. As I moved through my teenage years, I began to question most of what I had been taught about God. Was it possible that he could be found outside the Episcopal church? Was he present in all denominational churches? Even the ones that were not Christian? I knew in my heart that the answer to all of these questions was, yes, the spirit of God could be found in all churches and beyond all churches. I felt that he lived in my heart, and wherever my loving heart chose to carry him, there he was. As an adult, while I did attend church occasionally, my relationship with God became private and personal. I had reached the place in my heart where I knew that, for me, I could speak to God anytime, anyplace, no church necessary. In my forties, I began to seek God in a more spiritual way. I spent several years studying other spiritual practices and religions of the world in hopes of finding the truest, most perfect way to connect to God. In the end, I came to my conclusion, my epiphany, that the way we choose to worship God, the divine, is not so important. What is important is that we, as human beings, learn to love one another and serve one another, and how we choose to love and serve is up to us. It is our gift to God. All of my searchings led me back to this one simple truth, a truth that I had held in my heart all along.

During this spiritual quest, I read many books written by those who had experienced near death, as well as those who experienced open communication with the divine through prayer and channeling of the spirit. These were everyday people having extraordinary encounters with the divine. My spirit soared at the possibility of such a direct communion with God. In my heart, I knew that all things were possible with God. If he chose to allow such experiences to happen in order to fulfill his purposes, then would it not be true that they could happen to anyone?

Perhaps it was my open mind, my open heart, and my desire for communion that opened the door. I did not know for sure. All I knew for sure was that, once the door opened, I had to give myself permission to walk through it. Was God accepting me as I truly was, addictions and all? Was she saying that I was good enough to receive this gift? Was this experience truly meant for me, or was this some sort of mistake?

The truth was that I had yet to realize the magnitude of God's love for me. The divine plan that was beginning to unfold was the perfection that only God could create. My mind, body, and spirit were about to be released from the bondage of addiction and set free in a way I could never have dreamed possible. A love so powerful that it had the power to heal all wounds would heal me. My spirit was ready to soar and so it began.

With brave wings, I flew.

CHAPTER SIX

THE CONVERSATION BEGINS

On the afternoon of August 26, 2010, my extraordinary experience began. With a heavy heart, I was praying and asking God for help and guidance with a difficult family situation. As I prayed, a tremendous sadness entered my heart, and I began to weep. In an instant, my arms moved to squeeze my chest. To my surprise, I realized I was giving myself a hug. What was happening? I knew these arm movements had not come from me. Then the message came:

"I am always here with you"

"Mother in Heaven"

"Mother at Home"

My spirit immediately understood that these words were from my mother, and there was no fear or doubt as I received them. As the words flowed, so did the love and pure joy. As I received each word, I could feel the power and purity of her loving soul in my mind, body, and spirit. The magnitude of this love for me felt far greater than any love we had shared while she was here on earth.

I did not hear this message in my head as an audible voice. I received the words through my fingers. As the words flowed to me, the fingers on my right hand slowly traced each letter until it formed a word. The words flowed into sentences, and the sentences flowed to create the message. Tracing each word was effortless, requiring little energy on my part. The power that was present and moving my fingers was not from me. I let go and let the spirit of love send its message. As this pure, loving energy flowed into me, I could feel my spirit taking charge of the process. It helped my mind and body to receive, remember, and record each word.

Later, as the messages continued to come, I came to call this gift my "spelling from God." I did not understand why, but I knew that it was God who was allowing this exchange to take place and that it was, indeed, a gift for me, as well as my mother. The spelling was my secret joy, and in the beginning, I shared this secret with no one. I awoke each morning with indescribable joy and anticipation, looking forward to what message might come. If she came, what would my mother want to say to me today? What love and joy might her next message bring?

As the messages came, I began to understand that my mother was watching over me and was very much aware of what was going on in my life. For several weeks, I had been praying and asking for guidance that would lead me in the direction I needed to go. I had a decision to make, and it involved a family member who was in trouble and needed my help. I was very concerned about the sacrifices I would have to make if I chose to allow this person to move in with me. I knew it would change my life completely. I did not feel ready to make this commitment and had little support from my family to do so. My extended family chose to remain disconnected from the situation. I was afraid. I was looking for reassurance that, if I chose the path of love, I would be supported by God in all ways, even if the rest of my family chose differently.

On August 28, with these thoughts swirling in my head, my mother came to me again. She brought the following message:

"Watch what you can do with earth matters."

"Open ears matter."

"CDs talk to you. Be open to them."

"I love you all."

"Mother at Home."

Her next message came on August 30. I could feel a loving presence but was not sure if it was my mother, so I began the conversation with a question. This was the first time we had a real exchange where I asked questions and she answered them.

"Who am I speaking with?"

"Mother in Heaven."

"What should I do to help Anne?"

"Pray over her."

"Should I go visit her soon?"

"No."

"Is there anything else I can do other than pray?"

"Tell her that you love her."

"Is there anything else you want to say to me?"

"I love you all always"

As the message ended, I could feel her presence fading away. I was left wanting more. I asked myself the question: Was God somehow monitoring and guiding this communication between my mother and I? Without the presence of God, was it even possible?

If this were a gift from God, why was he allowing this to happen? For what purpose were the messages coming through? I chose not to ask these questions because I was not sure I wanted to hear the answer. I focused only on my desire for the communication to continue between my mother and me. I allowed all these other thoughts to fade away.

I chose not to share these experiences with anyone. I made this decision for several reasons. I was afraid that my family might not believe me and that their disbelief would negate my beautiful experiences. I was also afraid that, if I allowed this incredible gift to be opened up to the judgment of others, then it would be tarnished in some way. It would no longer be my special gift. I would not allow that to happen. My gift would not be taken away.

I intuitively knew that these exchanges between my mother and me were not some random occurrence that God was allowing because he loved me. I also understood that, at some point, I was going to be asked to bring a gift of my own into this story, something of great value to me. I would be asked to bring it into this triangle of love and lay it down. I could feel that this surrender was coming, but that was in the future, and I was joyfully existing in the now.

During September, there were several more communications between my mother and me, all concerning my sister. For privacy reasons, I have chosen to leave them from this story. For the most part, the communications with my mother were full of love and emotional support for me and what was going on in my life. Sometimes, we just enjoyed being together, choosing to relive happy memories. I understood that we could only meet in a space of love, and that, I learned, was the way through to each other. Love was the force that opened the door and allowed us to meet again. Even though we never spoke of her death and its debilitating effects on me, I could feel so much unresolved grief and trauma being healed through our conversations. I was so grateful to God for everything that these conversations were bringing to me.

As the days passed and time moved forward, I discovered that, yes, indeed, there was a purpose to the sending of the messages. It was a purpose that only God, in her infinite love for me, could have created. A metamorphosis was waiting for me, and my spirit was ready and waiting expectantly for the transformation to begin. I did not know what God's love would bring, but I was ready for it to arrive.

And so it did.

Chapter Seven

The Conversation Continues

On the afternoon of October 2, the next communication came. It arrived while I was reflecting on the events that had occurred earlier in the day. I had attended my youngest son's regional swim meet. It had been a highly emotional event for the swimmers and their families since the results would determine who would qualify for the upcoming state meet. My son had trained hard mentally and physically to get to this point in his swim career. My husband and I joined the rest of the parents, students, and coaches to cheer the team on.

My mother and my son had developed a close bond during the last four years of her life. He often traveled with me to visit her at the nursing facility. They enjoyed each other's company and shared lots of laughter together. I believe that when she died, the connection they shared did not die but lived on.

Before the meet began, as I was praying for my son and his team, I asked my mother to come and be present with her love and support. At the beginning of each race, I positioned myself at the end of the pool, facing his lane. At the start of each race, as my son began to swim, I could feel my mother's presence. I felt her next to me but also in the water with him too, sending us both incredible energy and love.

Later that day, I was alone, relaxing on the sofa in my living room when my hand began to trace these words. They were from my mother.

"Swim meet."

"Pictures."

"Won."

"Yea."

"Did you hear me calling to you to come watch the meet and help us win?"

"Yes."

"Will you be with us at the state meet next Saturday?"

"You can call me. You can always call me."

"I love you all always."

"Mother in Heaven."

On October 4, the following message came spontaneously: “Always remember to embrace life and to be true to everything you do.”

I wanted to ask a question about her passing and felt it was alright to do so. I asked the question, “When your body died, was it difficult for your spirit to pass over?”

“Everyone raptures.”

“I elevated to heaven.”

“Tell everyone to always tell the truth about themselves.”

“I love you all.”

“Mother in Heaven”

On October 19, as I was praying for guidance, my mother came again. I was desperate to make a decision about what, if anything, I should do for my sister. I asked my mother for help in making this decision, and these were the words she gave me:

“Bring her home.”

“Your brother does not understand that you care.”

"Anne has changed. She understands what she has done."

"You can pay for a sitter."

"Decide what you can do now."

"Pray."

"You always have a choice, but you will be sorry if you don't."

As I heard these words, I began to cry. I was overwhelmed with feelings of great love and sadness all at the same time. A flood of love washed over me. She gave me a few moments to finish with my tears and then she continued with her words:

"You can call me anytime."

"You can always call me."

"I love you all."

"Mother in Heaven."

As I traced these words, it felt as if she were standing right next to me, holding my hand and offering her loving support. It felt that way because she *was* there. I now understood that, if I called for her, she would always come. With these words, I knew that we had entered into a territory where I would never be without her presence again. How incredible would that be to live in a space where no one dies and takes their love with them? I would rest my heart there. A space where love never dies.

Love remains, always.

Chapter Eight

Be Good to Yourself

October 19 was a special day for me. When I awoke that morning, I hoped to hear from my mother but had no expectations beyond that hope. Little did I know what was coming to me. God allowed another door to open. Through that open door, my spirit guide entered and began his communion with me.

My mother had come to me that morning, bringing her support and guidance. Later that afternoon, my guide brought his first message to me. I was sitting on my sofa, eyes closed, attempting to take a nap. All of a sudden, with no warning, my arms reached up and crossed over my chest. I was surprised to be receiving a loving hug, and I assumed it was coming from my mother. In the next moment, I felt my fingers tracing these words across my chest: "Everything will be OK."

The energy that was flowing with these words did not feel familiar. It felt different because the words were being traced faster and more forcefully. I began to feel uneasy because I intuitively knew that these words were not coming from my mother. I asked my mother if the message was from her, and she answered, “No. It is from your spirit guide.”

I immediately felt a calm reassurance, and my uneasiness dissolved. If my mother was aware of and part of this introduction, then I felt it had to be alright to continue. As I asked for his or her name to be spelled, he returned to me and gave me his name, “E-r-o-b.”

As soon as I finished tracing the letters of his name, I felt at peace with his presence. Any trace of uncertainty that remained was replaced with joy and anticipation of what gifts this spirit might bring to me. I felt certain that whatever came, it would be all good. He allowed me to begin the conversation with a question, “Are you male?”

“Yes”

“Erob is an unusual name.”

“It is my heavenly name.”

“Why are you contacting me now?”

“You are having a weak time. I will help you go to Florida.”

“Do you communicate with my mother?”

"Yes. It is easier to reach you when you speak to mother."

"You need to stop all smoking. I am here for you to call on love. Be good to yourself. You don't take care of yourself. Don't smoke. Be good to yourself."

"Note everything."

With this first conversation, our friendship began. For me, our relationship was about much more than just receiving messages and guidance. Erob proved to be a true and dear friend, always supporting me and lovingly guiding me through each day and the challenges that lay ahead. I could not have made it through the coming weeks without him. He was indeed my godsend, and I will be forever grateful to him.

On October 20, as I was waking up after a night's sleep, he spoke to me again, "You are tired. Rest today before your trip to Florida on Friday."

"Will you be with me on the trip?"

"No."

"Will you be watching?"

"Yes."

"Will you talk with me?"

"Yes."

"I am worried about this trip and about what to do for Anne."

"You are so sensitive about everything. You are so sensitive about Anne. You are too sensitive."

"I cannot answer questions about Susan's fortune."

"You cannot answer questions about my future?"

"No. I am not allowed. I can only guide."

"You are so sensitive. See friends. See friends."

"Erob."

The following morning, my mother came to me again. I could feel a presence with me but was not completely sure if it was her or Erob, so I asked the question, "Who am I speaking with?"

"Mother in Heaven."

"I spoke with my spirit guide for the first time."

"I know. Erob will watch you go to Florida. You will drive a lot. You will sit on the beach. You will soak up the rays. Have fun. You cannot watch Anne day and night. You will do a lot. Be careful. I love you all."

"Mother in Heaven."

As she finished her message, Erob joined us and said,

"Be strong. You will be pleased with the road ahead."

"Erob"

"Erob loves Susan."

As I allowed these words to soak into my heart, an incredible sense of peace and security washed over me. It felt like a flood of love pouring into me, and I knew that no matter what, Erob presence was here to stay.

Yes, everything was going to be OK.

Chapter Nine

You Are Always with God

Later in the day, both Erob and my mother returned separately to give more messages. Erob came first, and we began another discussion about his name.

"I am not sure that I'm pronouncing your name right."

"Is it Ir-ob?"

"Yes. Do you like it?"

"Yes. It sounds like a Middle-Eastern name."

"No."

"It's your heavenly name?"

"Yes. It was given to me by God."

"I have always believed that there is a Mother God and a Father God."

"Yes, but it is Father God who draws names. Questions?"

"What can you tell me about heaven?"

"It is a better place than Susan's world. Susan's world cannot see delusions. You see sadness everywhere all the time. You see human beings cannot see joy all over the world. Teach, so you can bring God questions for all when you see beings. Susan is not seeing joy for mankind to print.

"All Susan sees is pain. Cannot see joy. You are not being joyful about your life. Susan cannot see joy. Susan cannot see joy. Susan cannot see everything beautiful. You see pain. You are everybody's pain. Susan is present in pain. See God. See God in you and in all you do. You are always with God. Tell."

"Susan is a prism."

"Erob loves Susan."

"You are a prism."

After receiving this message from Erob, my mother returned to share some final advice before my departure for Florida.

"Anne does not understand why she has been abandoned by her family. Go see her and tell her that you forgive her and love her. You are sorry. She is insane. Delusional."

"Are you telling me that the situation has changed? You told me before to go and get her and bring her home. Now you want me to visit and tell her I love and forgive her?"

"Yes. I don't think she can leave. She is waiting for love and forgiveness, and perhaps, her spirit is ready to go. Her mind is no longer there."

"Will she get sick and die?"

"No. She will surrender when ready. She is not ready until she has made peace."

"Are you saying that she can will herself to die when she's ready?"

"Yes, and I will be waiting for her."

"You are sorry for misjudging her behavior. Tell God."

As these words entered my mind and then sank into my heart, a tremendous sorrow began to swell in me. I saw all too clearly what she wanted me to see. The tears came quickly and hard. As the pain was flowing through and out of my heart, I heard her speaking to me.

"Everything will be OK."

"Everything will be OK."

"Everything will be OK."

"Be strong."

"I love you."

"Mother in Heaven."

I lovingly carried my mother's and Erob's words with me, as I walked into the next chapter of my story. I did my best to be strong against pain and only see the joy and beauty in all circumstances. I did my best to see God in all circumstances. I did my best not to judge another person's behavior because things aren't always as they seem. We see what's on the surface and rarely what lies beneath in the heart. These lessons were sometimes painful, but for me, essential. They carried me, step by step, through the storms that were to come and into the miracles waiting beyond.

And no matter what, I was always with God.

Chapter Ten

I Feel What You Feel

Six days later, on October 27, I returned home after seeing my sister. God was with me as I traveled to Florida. God was with me as I visited my sister, who was in a nursing facility. God was with me as I said good-bye and told her she could not leave with me. God was with me as she cried and raged. God was with me as I drove home full of shame, guilt, and grief. No amount of alcohol could erase these emotions and memories. They were deeply etched into my mind and body and covered my entire heart. They were a heavy weight I would carry with me as I moved forward. Where was the joy and beauty in this picture? I saw and felt nothing but pain.

Anne was no longer able to care for herself. Her brain damage was the result of many years of intense, chronic drinking. The damage from her alcoholism had wiped out her short-term memory and was permanent. Her condition made her appear to be like someone with Alzheimer's, except she was only forty-nine years old. She needed full-time care and supervision, and at that time, I was not prepared to take on such a responsibility. The irony of God asking me to face and deal with such a tragedy due to alcoholism was not lost on me. I understood what I was being shown. I saw no beauty. I saw no joy.

The pain and grief Anne was calling for me to help her carry seemed unbearable. Or was it God who was asking me to pick up the pieces, the pain and grief of alcoholism and carry them for her? Either way, I felt stuck in extreme pain with no way out. These were the feelings I carried back home with me, as I tried to return to my normal life. I did my best to reject the grief and guilt when it demanded to be heard. I tried to focus on the positive and trust that God would either take care of the rest or lead me to what I needed to do. It was a daily struggle to not give in to the despair that was always lurking, ready to attach itself to me if given a chance.

While I was in Florida, Erob came to me whenever I called. He came, offering support and love, and never once judged my actions or emotional responses to what I was facing. Even though I was not able to face it all with grace and acceptance, I did the best I could. I survived it all.

One evening, after my return, I was relaxing and allowing my mind to rest from all worry and anxiety.

I was immersed in watching a TV show when Erob came and began this conversation:

"I am Erob. I am your spirit guide. I see you watching TV, and I see you laughing. Erob smiles and laughs."

"Are you saying you feel what I feel?"

"Every time. Pray for Anne."

"I am sorry."

"I feel too sad for you when you feel sad."

"I will try to feel better. I am sorry."

"Be positive. Cell phone is something good for you to communicate with everyone."

"You go to sleep. You are tired. Turn off the TV and go to sleep. Don't see TV. See sleep. Sleep. Sleep. Sleep."

"When I am tired, does that make you feel tired?"

"Yes, I feel tired. Please go to sleep."

"I'm sorry."

"I love Susan."

"Erob."

"You have questions?"

"No."

"Go to sleep."

As I absorbed the spirit of love attached to these words, I felt myself being gently lifted and held in God's grace. My spirit was saying to me that God will give you the love and support you need to see you through all of this. She will be present with you as you face whatever each new day brings. God was not asking me to carry more than I could because she was carrying for me what I was unable to lift, hold, and carry myself. What love and peace I felt as I drifted off to sleep. God's grace, God's love—I knew in my heart that nothing else would do.

I needed nothing else to see me through.

Chapter Eleven

I Have Some Questions

The next day, Erob returned for more conversation. Our talks were becoming more relaxed. I felt comfortable asking him some curious questions about the spiritual dimension in which he lived as well as his purpose in my life.

"Who am I speaking with?"

"Erob."

"I have some questions."

"OK."

"What is your mission or job?"

"To guide you through life and see you home."

"What are my lessons to learn?"

"To learn knowledge and practice ESP. To seek knowledge to learn. Master seeks knowledge to learn. Erob seeks master to learn. Susan seeks master to learn. Teach ESP to be a guide. All I teach."

"Are you saying ESP is all you teach or you teach ESP to all?"

"ESP is all I teach."

"So you are my teacher?"

"Yes."

"You said before that you are my spirit guide."

"All."

"So you are both?"

"Yes."

"Are there other lessons I'm supposed to learn?"

"Yes."

"Are you supposed to help me learn them?"

"Erob teaches Susan ESP."

"Do I have other guides that are teaching me lessons?"

"Yes."

"Why haven't I made contact with these other guides?"

"You send. I call them to you."

"I send what?"

"You send messages, and I tell others. Be careful who you speak to. Evil man is everywhere around you."

"Who is this evil man?"

"Evil man is bad spirit. I always see evil man. Evil man is always around you."

"Should I be afraid?"

"No."

"Why not?"

"Because you are not evil, and he is evil. He seeks evil."

"So he cannot interfere when I talk to you?"

"No."

"Then why did you tell me to be careful who I speak to?"

"Because evil man is cunning and evil."

"So you cannot tell me what other lessons I'm here to learn?"

"No."

"Can the other guides tell me?"

"Yes"

"Can you ask them?"

"Yes."

"You are here to learn love and forgiveness. Another guide says you are here to learn temperance. Another guide says you are learning to make decisions about what you want to do for the rest of your days."

"Address what you want to know."

"I can't ask questions about my future, right?"

"You learn, and knowledge will come to you."

"Can I speak directly to the other guides?"

"Yes. Erob will call on them."

"Am I allowed to ask their names?"

"Yes. Pesyen, Buxad and Torene."

"Any more?"

"No."

"So I have three guides plus you as a teacher and guide?"

"Yes."

"Have we talked too long or do you want to continue?"

"Continue."

"Why was I chosen to learn ESP?"

"You were chosen because you see all sensory perceptions and because you read about it. You are so sensitive to everything. Susan is so loving and kind. Susan is special because she forgives. Forgiveness is love, and love is forgiveness."

"Talk later. You are tired."

"Erob."

As I reflected on my questions and their answers, I felt a sense of joyful anticipation. I knew these conversations had a divine purpose, which I did not yet understand. What were the possibilities for where this could go? What was I going to be asked to do? I felt no fear or anxiety because each time Erob and I spoke, love was present. When love is present, there can be no anxiety or mistrust. Where love is present, there is only faith in God's plan. I was safe in the hands of God. What a perfect place to trust and just let go.

And so, I let go.

Chapter Twelve

Take a Prayer

As the channeling of love continued, God was always present. I could feel his presence each time Erob and I spoke and, therefore, still at peace with the messages as they were channeled to me. I was beginning to trust all that was appearing in my life, knowing in my heart that God was the source of it all.

For several weeks, I had been experiencing channeled energy work. This was something I had read about but never experienced until now. As I rested, lying in bed, my hands began to move spontaneously over parts of my body. I was not the source of this energy nor was I controlling the movement of my hands. I was intrigued by this experience but not afraid. I watched in fascination as my hands made sweeping and circular motions across my torso and head. I intuitively knew that the source of this energy was divine, and the purpose was for some type of healing. Since I trusted the source, I just let the experience happen. It was after one of these healing sessions that Erob came to me and began the following conversation:

"The source was God."

"What was the purpose of the hand movements and gestures?"

"Healing."

"Was I correct in the movements?"

"You see errors so perfect to some. A great many people see Susan get spelling. Everyone sees Susan's spelling. Don't be afraid to spell. Questions?"

"Do I need your help with hand movements for healing? Am I doing effective healing on my body?"

"Susan is doing healing."

"How often should I do this healing to stay healthy?"

"Susan is not healthy."

"Are you saying that I am physically ill?"

"No."

"What are you saying?"

"Susan stays healthy by not smoking and by not drinking."

"So energy work is not something I should do on a regular basis?"

"Susan smokes too much and drinks too much."

"I know. I am going to try to do much better. Anything else?"

"Please eat something tonight."

"Anything else?"

"Everyone sees Susan's spelling to get special thoughts."

"Be safe Susan."

"Erob."

A few moments later, Erob returned and began speaking again:

"Susan seems sad."

"Tonight?"

"Yes."

"I am not sad. My son is home tonight."

"Sometimes Susan seems sad."

"Not sometimes. More often."

"Pray."

"I do."

"Pray more."

"Susan prays so she's not sad. Pray. Take a prayer. Take a prayer before you sleep. Don't drink. Be positive."

"Erob."

I was beginning to understand that the messages that were being given to me were not coming solely from Erob. They were messages from God that were being passed through Erob to me. So it was not just Erob that was speaking to me about my addictions, but God herself was saying it was a problem. I did continue to take a prayer, but I also continued to drink and smoke.

I did not know it then, but this conversation with Erob would be the last message that was recorded in my journal. In the coming weeks, I would become so immersed in miraculous events that I would not have the desire or time to record anything. Another shift had come. I was no longer the scribe recording the story, I *was* the story.

Erob and I continued to communicate for another week. During this time, he was guiding me and encouraging me to move forward and fulfill my promise to God. This was definitely not the end of my story. In many ways, it was just the beginning. The best and the worst was yet to come, and through it all, I always remembered Erob's words to take a prayer.

And so I did.

Chapter Thirteen

Amazing Grace

On the morning of October 31, Erob came to deliver a message to me. I did not feel the shift coming, but upon hearing his words, I knew it had arrived. I was informed that a decision had been made to stop all communication between myself, my mother and Erob. The communication could no longer continue because I had made no commitment to remove alcohol and cigarettes from my life. I was continuing to abuse my mind, body, and spirit and, therefore, making no effort to purify these parts of myself. I was not loving what God had so lovingly created. I was making no effort to love myself. My resistance to releasing my addictions was blocking my moving forward. Moving forward to what? I did not know. I was not told and I did not ask.

My response to this news was heartbreaking despair. I felt this emotion in my entire being. My mind, body, and spirit took the message and tried to make sense of it. How could this be? Why wasn't this explained to me before? I felt like I had been given the most perfect gift ever created and then told that, due to my choices, I would not be allowed to keep it. My mind was saying, "Can we not just start over and try this again?" My heart was sad and silent. I could feel my entire body begin to tense up, as fear and anxiety began to flow in. How would I be able to continue knowing that I would never be able to hear from my mother and Erob again?

I knew one thing for sure. For the first time in my life, I had been given the joy of experiencing a continuous flow of divine love. It had been mine, a never-ending flood of love flowing to me. There was nothing I would not do to keep this love. I was prepared to do anything, including releasing the drinking and smoking. Erob felt what was in my heart but said nothing. I was left with the feeling that the decision was final and, therefore, not negotiable.

I don't remember much about the rest of the day, but I do remember carrying the weight of Erob's words with me. I carried the heavy despair with me into the evening hours. I chose to hide all of this from my family. Tears were shed when I was alone and no one was watching. No one saw or knew of my despair except those in heaven who loved and watched over me. They, I knew, saw it all. They saw, felt, and heard my despair.

Later, that same evening, Erob returned to speak with me again. He came to deliver an unexpected message that would bring tremendous joy and relief. He came to deliver God's grace. He explained to me that if I chose to stop drinking and smoking immediately, the communication would be allowed to continue. I asked no further questions. With no hesitation or resistance, I responded with a "Yes!" As I spoke this word, I could feel my heart melt in gratitude and peace. As I spoke this word, I could feel another door opening, and I knew that, when I stepped through this door, there would be no turning back. I had no fear because I knew that I would be loved and supported through whatever lay ahead. I was surrendering, and it was so easy. This moment did not require great faith because, in my heart, I felt that wherever I was going and whatever I would be asked to do, God would be with me. I would be held in love and protected in a field of divine grace all the way through.

It was amazing grace.

Chapter Fourteen

You Know My Heart

God knew my heart so well. She created the perfect scenario for my redemption. She knew that I would joyfully step into this act, and my heart's desire would lead me toward freedom. There would be no options for failure. Love would see to that.

The next morning, November 1, Erob was by my side as we began to piece together our plan. He assured me that I would be assisted in the process of detoxing from alcohol and cigarettes. My last drink was on October 30, so all drinking had stopped. We had nothing there to discuss. I had no fear, only excitement and determination to see freedom from alcohol and cigarettes that I never thought possible.

For me, the plan for stopping smoking would be more challenging. I had always used cigarettes as a pacifier for anxiety, so I was more fearful of withdrawal from cigarettes than alcohol. How would I handle the anxiety if it came with the craving to smoke? Would God remove that too? I asked Erob if I could cut down gradually over the next five days instead of stopping immediately. He said, "Yes," but stated that it would be safer to stop all at once. When I asked why, he replied, "The Evil One will be around, watching and waiting for an opportunity to interfere." Even as I heard these words and felt his concern for me, I knew my anxiety would need to be pacified. I still chose to continue with my countdown plan to reduce the amount of cigarettes each day until I reached zero. This plan gave me a small sense of control over my anxiety, and for that, I was grateful. Following this plan, my last cigarette would be Thursday, November 6.

Looking back, I can clearly see the irony of it all. My anxiety demanded that I have some control over this process at a time when I needed to surrender completely. I was being asked to let go and trust that God knew what was best for me. Obviously, I did not walk the path in total faith and surrender, but God understood and, in his grace, allowed me to do part of it my way. I have since forgiven myself for this choice to give in to my anxiety in order to walk what I believed to be the safer path. I was allowed to learn my lesson my way. In the end, I learned that all good and wise choices are made from a place of love and faith, never anxiety or fear.

I moved easily through the next couple of days. Erob watched over and supported me as I worked the plan. The effects of alcohol withdrawal had not come, and

I was feeling confident and secure with everything. I believed that I would be protected from any and all harm and I rested my spirit in that faith. As the days passed and I gradually let go of the cigarettes, I began to feel joyful anticipation for the release that was coming. I still had no clear vision of how the story of my release would unfold. All I knew was that my life was about to shift again, and I was not only ready but excited to see where it was going.

On Wednesday, November 5, everything changed. My excitement turned to fear as my perfect plan began to unravel. I had planned to smoke two cigarettes that day, one in the morning and one in the evening, and then on Thursday, I was to smoke my final cigarette. As I sat on my front porch smoking my morning cigarette, Erob came to deliver an urgent message. He said, "The Evil One is all around you. You need to stop all smoking now. It is not safe for you to continue until tomorrow."

I listened to the message, but I did not ask any questions. I heard Erob's words. I felt his concern and trusted that what he was telling me was the truth of the situation. I felt guided and protected. I cannot say that I understood what was happening, but I felt the need to respect what I was being told. There were unseen forces, much more powerful than me, that were beginning to manifest in my story. I did not smoke another cigarette that day, nor did I ever smoke again. That part of my life was over. It was finished.

I anxiously waited for the next shift to begin. I could feel its presence, but I had no idea what was coming to me. My spirit reminded me that God was creating my path to freedom, so there was nothing to fear. God knew my heart, and that was all I needed to know. Love and guidance would be with me and my spirit as we walked the path.

So, stepping forward, we began to walk.

Chapter Fifteen

I Surrender

As I began my surrender walk, I stepped inward into my own little universe where God was waiting for me. I never felt more loved. I asked for nothing. I had no desires or expectations other than wanting and expecting the divine dialogues to continue. Of course, I was grateful for the protection that surrounded me and wanted it to stay in place. It had been Erob and God orchestrating the events that led me here. Now, it was only the presence of God and me together in this space. Erob was no longer with us. Without being told, I knew he had finished his assignment with me and was leaving. I did not know if and when I would speak with him again.

The addictions that I had so closely guarded and coveted for over three decades had been left behind, dissolved into nothingness. The weight had been lifted. God had disposed of what I no longer needed. My addictions were no longer mine to carry. My spirit was now free. My mind and body would soon follow my spirit into this beautiful new freedom. The transformation had begun, but it would not be easy to see it to completion. I was grateful to God for only allowing me to see one step at a time of what was to come. I have no written record of this chapter of my story. I have no journal entries to refer to for accuracy. I am writing what I remember in the sequence I remember it happening. I do know that there are gaps in time when I have no clear memory of what was happening to or around me.

During the day, I was alone. My husband was at work, and my son was at school. In the evenings, they were involved in their own activities, so I was alone most evenings as well. What they did witness, we did not discuss. They had no understanding, only fear, as they watched some of these events unfold. I chose not to reach out to friends because I was afraid that they would not believe me, and besides, what could they do to help? As God would have it, I received no calls or visits from friends during this time.

I remember the events that for me were the most significant. From beginning to end, this chapter lasted about ten days. During this time, my mind and body began to cleanse itself. Every organ, every tissue, and every cell were directed to release its poisons. I was being rinsed clean through a flood of love. I was on my own but not alone. The presence of love was always with me. I understood that my mind and body were surrendering to the will of my spirit and that my spirit was resting with God.

Along with the love, God allowed anxiety and fear to be present as well. As much as I wanted God to take it all, he allowed me to experience the entire process of letting the poisons go, and that included experiencing the emotional, as well as the physical, effects of the release. I could feel that it was not going to be an easy surrender.

Too many years of abuse had caused my mind and body to become prisoners to my addictions. As I began to surrender, my mind and body became confused and resisted the release. Not understanding what was happening, the desire to hold onto the drugs was intense. Fear and anxiety came and stayed. They came and were my companions through the worst of it.

As the next few days passed, I felt as if my anxiety was running at full throttle. I had no desire to eat, and I have no memory of eating anything. Sleep did not come easily. My body felt as if it was in a fight or flight situation that never stopped. As my mind was surrendering to the will of my spirit, I could still function consciously in my everyday world, but I often found my mind shifting without warning into a different dimension. I felt as if I had one foot in my normal world and the other foot in the world of my spirit. My mind moved back and forth between the two worlds as needed. As my mind and body moved through this chaos, my spirit was always present with love and guidance. Some may say that my state of mind and my moving between dimensions to connect with my spirit were the result of hallucinations due to alcohol withdrawal. Yes, my mind was in chaos. It was screaming for the drugs because it knew no other way to function, but it was not a delusion. My mind was not hallucinating. It was experiencing the natural flow of the release of toxins, and the process was naturally chaotic and disorienting.

As I moved through the cleansing process, I experienced no physical cravings for alcohol or cigarettes. I felt that my spirit was responsible for giving me that grace. My spirit, always flowing with love, continuously merged into my mind and body. This love was always present. The more fearful I became, the more love I received. This love was what allowed me to endure and trust what was happening. If love was present, then God was present. God was there, allowing me to experience the cleansing process and loving me through it all. I rested my mind, body, and spirit in that truth. It was what gave me the strength and the enduring faith to face what was coming and to complete my surrender.

And so, I released my grip on
everything and just let go.

Chapter Sixteen

The Evil One Is All Around

As I was moving through my cleansing process, my normal existence began to fade away. Time seemed to stand still, as everything inside of me and around me continued to shift and change. It was in this lapse, this stillness, that the real drama began to unfold. When the Evil One arrived, I did not know where to go or what to do, but I prayed God's grace and protection would see me through.

I felt the presence of the Evil One for the first time on Thursday evening. He presented himself as an invisible force, bringing with him the emotions of extreme fear and dread that were so powerful, I could feel them in every part of my mind and body. I could not see his presence, only feel it. Later, as he became more powerful, he would sometimes announce his arrival with a slapping sound followed by a foul smell. He did not speak audible words to me but seemed to want to consume me through his negative emotions. For me, he felt like the complete absence of love. Each time he greeted me, he brought with him only fear and persecution. Although I had been warned about him and to be on my guard, I had received no lessons on how to act in his presence. I knew my spirit and the presence of God were with me, but I was receiving no direct guidance. I had no idea what this negative force wanted from me, but whatever it was, I knew it was not good.

From this moment forward and for the next ten days, he would appear without warning to torment me. When he had enough, he would retreat only to reappear later in the day. As each day passed, I could feel his energy growing larger and more powerful, as he passed his fear and dread onto me. He especially liked to come at night when I was totally isolated.

My husband was still choosing to stay away from what he could not understand and could not control. His fear and lack of understanding kept him from stepping in to comfort and guide me. Not knowing what to do for me or with me, he stepped aside and let the story unfold. When we did talk, my son and husband made their feelings clear about what was happening. They had no intention of participating in this drama of the unraveling of Mom's mind and body. They understood that they were helpless to protect me from a force that they could not see or hear, a force that might not even possibly exist. Their lack of support and understanding hurt me deeply and only served to fuel my anxiety and fear. At the time, I did not understand why the story needed to include such pain and feelings of abandonment.

As the story continued to unfold, I began to see his plan for what it was, and it terrified me to think he might succeed. The Evil One had declared war on my family, using fear and mistrust as his weapons. The love that had always thrived in our home was now being ripped apart. He was dividing and conquering our love and our connection to each other. It was the perfect scenario for him to accomplish his purpose. I was isolated with very little contact and no human intervention. No one was showing up to protect me, or so he thought.

As I prayed my way through each day, I was constantly on guard for the Evil One to present himself. I never knew when he was coming or what he might bring. I only knew that, when I felt his presence, I could think of nothing else but escaping the scene of terror. My first thought was, "Where can I hide to be safe?" Later on, when I realized hiding was useless, I tried to put as much distance as possible between us. It became an impossible game of cat and mouse. The fear that was always surrounding me, always watching and waiting was beginning to consume me.

There was a story that was placed in my mind at this time. I do not know if my fears placed it there or if the

Evil One projected it into my mind. I do know that, for the next several days, the same scene repeated itself over and over in my mind, as I acted it out in my reality. I was being pursued by the Evil One. I understood his purpose. It was to capture my mind, body, and spirit and claim me as his own. I also understood that, if he won this battle, I would never again be in the presence of love and peace. I would never feel the presence of God again. I would be swallowed in anxiety and fear. The possibility of the stealing of my being was both terrifying and heartbreaking at the same time. I would do anything to prevent this from happening.

It was in this feeling of panic and desperation that I began to call out to Mother God for protection. I quickly learned that every time I called for her to come, she was there in an instant. I did not see her but always felt her calming, loving presence surrounding me with protection. When necessary, she would communicate loving, reassuring messages to me but always without spoken words. I heard and felt the words as she placed them in my heart. I was so grateful for her presence and for the love she brought to me.

When she arrived, armed with her love, the Evil One was forced to leave. I witnessed her incredible power, as waves of love flowed through me and flooded the space around me. There was no space left for anything but her love. The Evil One was forced to retreat, but hours later, he would come again. Since he could appear at any time, I was constantly on guard and anxious. At night, when rest was difficult, Mother God placed a light in the shape of a cross on my bedroom wall. This light was a reminder of her constant presence and protection. She was so faithful to me. Each and every time I called her name, she would arrive with her love and push him back again. He was persistent, but she was all-powerful. His evil was no match to the power of her love.

One evening, the Evil One arrived swelling with an incredibly powerful energy. I could feel him coming, and upon his arrival, I fell into a panic. My husband, feeling and seeing nothing, watched in disbelief as I grabbed my keys and ran out of the house toward my car. Every cell in my mind and body was electrified by fear. In my panicked mind, I was escaping, and my car was driving me to safety, but where was I going? As I sped down the dark driveway, I called out for Mother God to join me. I immediately sensed her peaceful presence next to me. I glanced at the seat and saw nothing, but I knew she was there. I felt her love begin to flow in and around me. This invisible love coaxed my body into relaxing a bit, even though the fear was still racing through my mind.

She did not direct me on which way to go, where to drive in order to escape the Evil One. She simply stayed with me and was present at every turn, every stop, every decision. If I reached an intersection and was unsure about which was the best way to go, she would calm me with her reassuring words: “Do not despair. You are safe.” In the presence of her love, I became strong and fearless. As we continued our drive, I began to trust myself to find my way through the maze of darkness and to return home safely. We left the Evil One behind us, lurking somewhere in that darkness, searching for me.

Once again, I felt the shift come over me. As the fear was flowing out of me, the love was flooding into my mind, body, and spirit. From this love flowed peace. The power of this love would see me through and take me home where I could rest in peace. I had been shown that the power was always mine if only I would call upon it.

And I would, indeed, call upon it again.

Chapter Seventeen

Rising Up

As the days continued to pass, I began to absorb the truth of what was happening to me. I made peace with the idea that it was not possible to hide from the Evil One. If that were true, then it made no sense to continue to try to run and hide. He was everywhere and could appear before me in an instant without warning.

The days and nights of clinging to Mother God for protection were over. In my heart and soul, I knew it was my destiny to find the strength and courage to take a stand against the Evil One. There was no way around it. If I was ever going to find peace, my only choice was to walk straight into this destiny and face my fears. My soul needed to declare its intentions to always remain with Mother and Father God and to walk the path of love, casting aside all my fears. I understood this all, yet I was still afraid. Afraid of what? Was I going to have to stand all alone, facing the Evil One with no protection, and for how long? I had no choice but to walk forward in faith, that God would be present and my love would not fail.

My stand against the Evil One began one evening when he arrived for his nightly visitation. This visit felt unusual, and I sensed that it would not be like the rest. There would be no more of our running and hiding game. My instincts told me that he had arrived with the purpose of speaking directly to my soul. He had words to speak to me, and it was time for me to stand still and listen. He was ready to claim me as his own. His desire was to declare victory over me and the goodness that I had come to represent. I understood that, if I lost this battle, there would be no turning back, no second chances. Every part of me—my mind, body, and soul—would be his to use for his purposes, and I would be left alone in my fear and despair. All of the love, peace, and joy God had brought into my life would dissolve and disappear. I would lose my freedom and return to a life of bondage.

As I was standing in my bedroom, facing a force I could not see, I felt Mother God's presence move into place alongside me. A moment later, I felt Father God's presence move to my other side. With their arrival came the love and protection that I felt I so desperately needed and wanted. The three of us stood facing the presence of the Evil One. Two all-powerful, invisible forces were on either side of me and another in front of me.

I could feel the power of the rage, fear, and despair that was multiplying and flowing from the presence of the Evil One. As this energy moved toward me, I felt no fear because, at the same time, this energy was being met by the tremendous wave of love and peace flowing and expanding throughout the room. At that moment, my mind and body began to relax a little, as my spirit eagerly stepped forward to speak its destiny.

Mother and Father God communicated to me that the purpose of the gathering was for all to hear my declarations and intentions. I was told that no spoken words would be necessary because I would speak from my heart. Even though I was feeling some anxiety about choosing the right words, I also felt that, if I stumbled, the love that was present would carry me through any confusion or uncertainty. There seemed to be an unspoken understanding between them as to how they would proceed. To me, it felt like they had done this many times before and would continue to do so. I, on the other hand, was in the dark, not knowing what was coming next.

The Evil One began with a discourse on the state of my soul, including every selfish, unloving choice I ever made in my life. As he presented one after the other, it seemed as if all of my sins were flowing endlessly in a stream of darkness right in front of my eyes. Worst of all, as I heard his words, I knew that every word coming from him was the truth. I did not feel shame, but fear began to rise up once again. Fear that, in the eyes of God, I would not be good enough to stand in the light. If that were true, there would be no love, peace, and redemption for me. He spoke the evidence that showed I did not deserve to stay with love. He reminded me of all the times I chose fear instead of love; all the times I chose despair over peace. And where was my faith? According to the history of my choices, the way I had chosen to live my life, I did not belong with God. I belonged with him.

The Evil One stated that I would not continue to be free of my addictions because, for decades, I had willingly chosen enslavement to them. Each day I had chosen to defile my mind, my body and my spirit, and I had willingly accepted the consequences of doing so. I had even enjoyed it. I had chosen to destroy what God had created for his purposes. I had chosen to worship my addictions. Therefore, I had chosen to worship him, not God. I had been at peace with living in darkness for too long for it to be otherwise.

When the dark words finally stopped flowing, God's light moved in front of me. I could still feel Mother God's presence as a sweet peace came over me. God began to speak light into every dark word the Evil One had spoken about me. For every sin the Evil One had listed, God spoke of two choices I had made in my life that were kind, loving, and selfless. As God spoke, every word melted into my heart and released a surge of strength into my soul. As he finished, I felt myself being lifted and held in the strength and power of his love to a space where there was no room for shame. I realized, for the first time, that I had been forgiven for everything.

In the next moment, I heard Mother and Father God speaking to me. They made it clear to me that they could no longer protect me from the Evil One and his attacks. In order for him to leave, I would have to stand and speak my truth to him. He would listen, and if convinced, he would retreat, and the attacks would stop. Mother and Father God continued to stand beside me but only as silent witnesses. My power would be in my words, and so I began to speak fearlessly and truthfully from my heart. These were the words I spoke:

"You are wrong about my soul. I am pure light and full of God's love because my mistakes have been forgiven, and now I am washed clean by the healing grace of God. I am created anew because I have chosen to stand with God in the light. This is who I am now, and this is who I shall remain always. I will not return to your darkness. I do not belong with you because you are the absence of all the love that I am. I will no longer run away from you in fear. I will stand firmly in my faith that I am loved always and forgiven for any faithless, loveless choices that I may make. As long as I return to the light and ask for forgiveness, God's love will always remain

with me. I am allowed to choose. I have been created for this moment, for this choice.

"I choose God."

When I finished speaking, there was only silence. The Evil One said nothing. His presence began to fade, and as he left, all my fear, anxiety, and shame went with him. There was nothing and no one left in the room except me, standing in peace, embraced by the light of the divine.

I had risen up, and I was free.

Chapter Eighteen

Learning to Pray

One more chapter of my story was complete, and a new one was beginning. I was free of the Evil One, but God was not finished with me yet. From the end of November 2010 until January 2011, my miraculous transformation continued with many lessons along the way. My husband and son, grateful that this chapter was over, moved forward with their normal lives. Their busy schedules continued to give me the space and privacy I felt I needed to continue my communications with God. During the day, I was alone in my home, free to do as I pleased with no judging audience and no distractions. This was my time to learn whatever God had to teach me, and I was a ready and willing student.

Looking back, I believe that God arranged this space and time for us to be together. My friends still knew nothing about my experience and what was happening in my life. There seemed to be a distant space between us during this time. No one called to talk or came to visit. I did not know it, at the time, but one of my closest friends had been called out of state to be with her mother, who was seriously ill. She did not return for weeks or perhaps a month. I, for the most part, was alone and more than satisfied with this arrangement. I was joyful with all that was happening to me and was content to experience this time of total immersion into divine love.

Morning, noon, and night, I could feel God's love surrounding me. It was above me. It was below me. It was inside of me. It flowed ceaselessly to me. There was no end to this love. There was nothing I needed to do or be or say in order for my soul to receive it. It was a gift. I understood that it was my divine right as a soul in human form to receive this love. As the days passed, I came to realize that my mind, body, and spirit were being held in a field of divine love, a field of grace. Day after day, as this never-ending love continued to flow, I began to trust that it would stay with me and not leave.

God was recreating my mind, body, and spirit according to his will, transforming me into what he had always desired me to be. Every morning when I awoke, I would sit quietly in my living room chair and wait for the presence of God to come. This chair became very special to me. I called it my God chair. I took great comfort and joy in knowing that, each time I placed myself in this seat, opened my heart, and waited patiently, God would come. Sometimes the wait was brief, and other times, it felt like I sat for hours. With the longer wait time, I would often feel myself slipping into a deep meditation. Each morning, as I waited for the communion to begin, I experienced the bliss of being saturated in God's love. In return, love poured from my heart back to God. When I felt the presence of the divine in the room and I began to hear his words in my heart and mind, I knew the daily lesson had begun.

My first lesson was a lesson in prayer. Through daily practice, God taught me the elements of true, connected prayer. I was shown the importance and power of holding my hands together palm to palm when I prayed. I was shown that my right hand represents and holds the energy of my mind and body, and my left hand holds the energy of my soul. When they are brought together in the prayer position, they form a channel through which my prayer can flow. When my hands come together and the fingers and palms of each hand are connected, the energies of love, faith, and devotion begin to flow through my fingers from my thumb to my little finger. These energies, as they come together, become a powerful stream that carries my prayer to God. As God receives my prayer, he then returns the same loving energy back to me, reversing the order of the flow. Through this exchange of energy, a powerful, connected prayer is created.

I felt, in my heart, that this love connection was a never-ending, flowing process that I could connect with at any time. I began to understand that I was the creator of my powerful prayers. The power of my prayers did not come from my words alone but from the love connected to and contained within my words. All I needed was my heart and my hands to send a prayer, and God was always present to receive it and return his love to me.

Along with this lesson, God began to speak to me about the content of my prayers. How I was praying was affecting how my prayers were received and answered. I learned that my needy prayers, full of anxious requests and begging for change to come were not always received with love and, therefore, not always answered with love. Prayers that were sent from my heart with the pure energy of love were received with love. When I asked for what I truly needed in my life, grace was given freely as I needed it, and it was always given in the spirit of love.

This was also true when I prayed for others. I learned that, while God hears all prayers, he answers them according to his will and purpose for each soul's experience. God may not choose to remove a painful event in a person's life, but they will always receive the love and grace to see them through. There is a purpose to each and every challenge in life. It is not for me to judge or understand why God is allowing an experience to take place. My role is to simply be present with the person and love them as they are going through their challenge. The love I offer must be unconditional and given with no expectations or desires attached to it. This pure, divine love has the power to heal all wounds. The sharing of this love is our service to God and to each other.

Next, I was taught the importance of always praying in truth. I learned that truthful prayers, sent in love, were powerful. They were received in love and answered in the best way possible. I was taught that, when I pray, I need to always speak the whole truth, not simply my version of the story that I want to present for my purposes. God wanted to hear the entire story in detail no matter how shameful or sad. As I was told many times, "The truth shall set you free." I recited those powerful words often and knew them to be true. They were a guiding light for me in so many ways.

As I was completing the lesson of praying in truth, God began to teach me a powerful lesson about praying in the spirit of forgiveness. I learned that every prayer must begin with asking for forgiveness for any actions or choices I had made that were not in the spirit of love. It did not matter to God if the act that needed forgiveness had been made one time or a hundred times. Each time I repeated the choice, I must ask for forgiveness before I was allowed to move forward with my prayers. As long as I spoke the truth and asked for God to forgive me, forgiveness was mine. Once forgiven, I was free to release any guilt and was able to receive God's love once again. I did not need to carry shame for my actions, only the joy of forgiveness and the promise to my spirit that, next time, I would choose love.

I was humbled by this lesson of forgiveness and amazed at God's compassion for me and my human weaknesses. Even though I kept score of my errors and counted in shame the number of times I repeated them, he did not. He gave his unconditional forgiveness every time because he loved me.

I learned to be careful of my thoughts because I knew my thoughts were where my anxiety began. My anxiety most often would lead to fearful choices. God understood it all. Nothing was hidden. I was taught that my spirit must not be weighed down by my poor choices. A thought, word, or action based on fear, instead of love, must be forgiven and then released. The slate needed to be wiped clean daily, if not hourly, in order for my mind, body, and spirit to remain in love. Anxiety and fear were not welcome, only love and faith. I was taught that I must always remember the loving-kindness and forgiveness that had been given to me and carry that forward to others who may need my forgiveness.

Along with the prayers of truth and forgiveness, I was shown the importance of praying in gratitude for all the love, support, and blessings that were flowing into my life. I was taught to ask for what I needed in each moment, believe that it was being given, and then pray a prayer in gratitude for the loving-kindness given to me. I was to be grateful for all God had allowed in my life, especially during challenging times. I learned that I would not always receive everything I asked for, but I would receive what was best for me at that moment, and it would always be what I needed in order to take the next step in my life. I did not need to understand or agree with what was being given to me through the grace of God. There was a purpose to everything in God's universe, even the most incredibly painful experiences. I learned to trust God, even when I did not understand why things were happening as they were and when I was hoping and praying for something different. When people or events came that caused me pain, fear, or despair, instead of being angry at the circumstance, I learned to be grateful that love was always with me, supporting and guiding me through to the end.

This time of learning to pray, for me, was a treasure I will always remember with such a sweet love in my heart. I was, and still am, grateful for it all.

As my prayer lessons were completed, I knew I was ready to begin the next phase of my transformation.

The foundation had been laid. I had learned to pray in truth, forgiveness, and gratitude and always with love in my heart. My communion with God would always remain strong and powerful, and with that truth firmly in place, I knew I was ready to take the next step wherever it would lead me. My love for God and with God had become a powerful force, and I had learned that, when great love is present, all things are possible. I was excited to see where this love would take me next. I could feel my mind, body, and spirit stepping forward and beginning to flow toward God and his purpose for me.

Joyfully, I followed the flow of love.

Chapter Nineteen

Learning to Honor My Body

During the time that God was teaching me the lessons of prayer, I continued to be held and supported by the Holy Spirit in so many ways. My mind and body were struggling and in need of healing. While I began the process of healing, mentally and physically, my spirit rested with God and was, therefore, at peace.

Over the course of a few weeks, my body had endured tremendous physical stress. High anxiety combined with no interest in eating had caused rapid weight loss. I had begun the process of cleansing my mind and body with no effort on my part. I could feel the years of toxic waste being released, and it felt good. Decades worth of alcohol, cigarettes, and their toxic chemicals were releasing and beginning to flow out of me. It felt as if I was being drained dry. I became like a sponge, waiting to make contact with water. How would God fill me up? I was waiting to be saturated with his love. Nothing else would do. Divine love would be in charge of teaching me how to care for my body in ways that would allow God's life force, his love to flow continuously through me.

I was assigned a teacher, another spirit guide, whose job it would be to teach me these lessons. His name was Shamoine, and he would remain with me for about six weeks. We did not communicate through conversation, as I had done with Erob. Shamoine made it clear to me that he was not interested in dialogue or any questions I might have. He simply gave commands or directions and then expected me to follow them. I did not need my spelling to communicate with him because he transmitted his words to me simply by placing them in my mind. I heard his voice clearly. There was no confusion with his words. I understood what he was asking of me each and every time. Step by step, he walked me through many difficult lessons. He did not teach me these lessons through instruction alone, but also through the experience of daily practice.

I understood that, if I was going to continue with the communion and my lessons, I would be required to let go and allow God to teach me his ways. My first lesson was to surrender my will completely. I needed to practice obedience in all things.

I learned to listen for the voice of Shamoine. When it came, I was to stop all that I was doing and then listen for his directions. The divine structured my day in a way that left little time or space for free will. Shamoine directed my steps and all of my actions as I moved through each day.

Once again, I did not feel comfortable sharing what was happening with family and friends. I was never told not to share this experience; I simply chose not to do so. I did not want their judgments, nor did I not want their interference. I was not going to let this experience be tarnished by anything that was not love. I knew they would not believe what was happening to me, so I chose to remain silent. If anyone asked what I was doing as I stopped, bowed my head, and listened for directions, I would say I was praying. Perhaps they did not believe me, but I was never challenged directly, so I was allowed to continue without interruption. Communication with Shamoine was easier when I was alone and could speak freely.

As time passed, I learned to adapt to this surrendering process and was able to move through each day in total obedience. Lessons came first. My desires and wants came second. I willingly gave myself to this process because the lessons were given in the spirit of love and because I understood that, in order for me to protect and maintain what God was creating in me, I had to learn new ways of caring for my body.

The first item on my agenda was nutrition. Since the detoxification process had already begun, I was well on my way to becoming the pure being Shamoine desired me to be. Everything that was not a pure, clean food or drink was eliminated from my diet. I was instructed to eat only whole foods, mainly, fresh fruits and vegetables. No processed foods were allowed. Anything that came packaged in a box or bag was no longer part of my daily diet. I was not to eat or drink anything containing sugar. I could no longer drink coffee or tea. Water would be my only drink.

I continued to have no cravings for alcohol or cigarettes. I did, however, greatly missed my morning coffee. When it was taken away, I felt deprived and, as a result, began to crave it. Throughout the entire lesson, which lasted weeks, I craved that one cup of morning coffee. I learned that the more I thought about that cup of coffee, the more powerful my cravings became, and the more powerful the cravings, the more obsessive and deprived I felt. I learned the power of a single thought and that I could choose acceptance and peace of mind instead. It was difficult to let the coffee go, but I learned that I could live without it.

As the lessons continued, I received instructions on which foods to purchase and how to prepare them. I even had a lesson on how to eat slowly and mindfully so that my body could digest food properly. My teacher guided me, as I shopped for groceries. He was with me, as I cooked, and was also with me, as I ate my meals. I often prepared separate meals for myself, since my husband and son were not interested in eating these foods. Some meals were eaten with family members, but often, the cooking and eating of meals were separate. I learned to accept whatever situation presented itself and to be at peace with the many times I ate alone. I tried to always go with the flow but still remain true to myself and my newfound goals.

I began to wrap my heart and mind around the idea that the purpose of consuming food was not for pleasure but to nourish my mind and body. If my mind and body were to be transformed into a healthy, balanced being, I knew I must continue to eat and drink only the foods that would give nourishment. I was taught to eat fruits and vegetables raw or only slightly cooked through steaming or sautéing. I was instructed to cook only the amount I would need for one meal. If there was any food left over at the end of the meal, I was to throw it away instead of storing it as leftovers for another meal. Shamoine explained to me that food should be eaten immediately after cooking while the nutrients and life force energy was still present. When food was cooked, stored, and later reheated, the vital energy was spent and little, if any, nutrition remained in the food.

At the start of each meal, I was instructed to sit quietly and relax for a few moments, then give thanks for the meal before beginning to eat. In this quiet moment, I also learned to think about the positive effects the food was going to have in my body. I learned to eat and be satisfied with smaller portions while giving my body the amount it needed and could easily digest. When I finished my meal, if I craved more food or still felt hungry, I was told that I was finished and that the meal was over. I learned to cook only the amount I would be allowed to eat.

For six weeks, I obediently followed Shamoine's instructions and practiced my lessons. Each day, as I cleansed my body inside and out, my body continued to shed more layers of accumulated toxins. As the poisons continued to flow out of my body, I began to feel lighter, cleaner, and more joyful. The lessons no longer felt like restriction and deprivation but more like guidelines for creating the clean, pure body I now desired.

When Christmas morning arrived, I was told I could enjoy one cup of coffee and one piece of coffee cake. What a treat that was! I savored every bite and every sip with joy and gratitude. When I finished the cake and coffee, I realized I did not want or need anymore. One cup and one piece were enough. It was perfect. Most things in moderation and some things not at all. Lesson learned.

Thank you, Shamoine, for teaching me to honor my body. I continue to carry these lessons forward.

With gratitude, I practice them as I was taught, remembering to honor what has so graciously been given to me.

My body as God created it to be.

Chapter Twenty

Renewing of the Mind

As the chemical toxins were being released from my mind, an unexpected challenge began to rise up and make itself known. Even though my prayers were strong in faith, negative, anxious thoughts were still being created in my mind in a way that worried me. Why were my anxious thoughts returning? I believed that the debilitating part of my life was over, yet here was the fear presenting itself again. Was this God's way of challenging me to live out my faith, not just in words but through actions? In the past, I would pacify and calm such thoughts by drinking to forget or smoking to calm the anxiety. Now that the alcohol and cigarettes were gone, would I be left to do battle with my fearful thoughts without God's help? That thought, in itself, made me anxious.

Once again, God's grace continued to flow into me. He began to teach me how to surrender these negative thoughts through prayer. I was shown that, as soon as an anxious thought enters my mind, I must pray to release it before it can claim any power over me. I must ask God to take the thought and then be willing to surrender it. Finally, I must claim, through faith, that God had received it and, in return, sent his peace, his reassurance that all was well. This surrendering process was not always easy for me, and it did not always have immediate results. I found that the stronger my anxious and fearful thoughts were, the more difficult it was to release them.

I learned that I must also pray to God to ask for help during the times when I felt weak and afraid, when my faith did not feel strong enough to face what was in front of me. As God helped me to strengthen my faith, then it was my turn to demonstrate this faith by declaring to myself and others that all was well. I had to believe in my heart the truth of the statement that all things were as they should be, as God intended them to be. If this statement was true, then there was no space in a faithful mind for anxious thoughts. No fear, No anxiety, only love and faith. In times of intense stress when anxiety was running high, I found I needed to pray this prayer repeatedly as many times as necessary until release and then relief came to bring me peace. God's grace to me.

I also learned that, when people and events in my life appear to be out of my control, I was to place them in the hands of God and then wait for instructions on what, if anything, my love could do to help. I was to always act from a place of inspiration, never from a place of fear or need to control.

I learned, through trial and error, how important it was to be mindful of my thoughts. I understood that thoughts were powerful, and I learned that when they were translated into words, they were even more powerful. I was shown the power of carrying a loving, faithful spirit in my mind and heart always, no matter what was presented to me. With this spirit, I began to learn to speak faith over my life and all things in it. All I needed was faithful prayer and God's presence for all to be well.

Releasing negative thinking and anxiety made room for love, faith, and joy to be present in my mind and that, for me, was the ultimate goal. To remain joyfully centered in the love of God and to realize that I had the power to place myself there at any time and under any circumstances was God's lesson for me. What a powerful lesson that was, and still is, for me. It is not always easy to have such faith, but in my heart I carry these words:

All things are possible to those who believe.

Chapter Twenty-One

The Never-Ending Prayer

One day, in January 2011, the communion door closed. I did not record the date because, at that time, I did not understand what was happening. I believed the silence that I was experiencing was just a temporary lull in communication, even though I had an uneasy feeling that something was different and not quite right. As the days turned into weeks, I began to realize that the divine voices may not return. By February, I knew that the conversations had ended. I could feel the distance and emptiness in the space between us. Even so, I continued to carry a small glimmer of hope. My heart was telling me what I did not want to hear. I had completed my lessons, and it was time for me to let go.

I felt abandoned. I did not understand how, without any warning or explanation, God could withdraw the channel of love. I felt as if I had been given the most precious gift I could ever receive and now it was being taken back. I longed to hear their loving words and feel their presence again. I heard and felt nothing but silence.

As February turned into March and March into April, I continued to ache for their return. I also began to face the reality that I might never again be granted the gift of direct communication with the divine. Even though I heard nothing but silence, I continued to pray and trusted that my prayers were being received. I began to search for the presence of God everywhere. I found nothing but me, longing to return to where I had been. God had returned to being a mysterious, silent, but ever-present force in my life.

If God in her infinite wisdom had allowed this channel of love to open for a purpose, then she was choosing to close it for a purpose as well. I began to look at everything from a larger perspective, and I had so many unanswered questions, What was I supposed to do with this experience? Did God want me to take my lessons, apply them to my life and move forward from here? Was I being asked to stand on my own without the love and support of my teachers and guides and especially my mother? Was I supposed to write and speak about this experience? How was I supposed to understand and make peace with all of this, if I had no voices to guide me and help me to understand? I could find no answers, and this confusion haunted me for months.

Over time, my spirit, in its ceaseless love for me, led me to an understanding that I had not been abandoned but had been set free. I had been set free to live my life according to the divine lessons that had been given to me. The lessons and the love were forever mine. These were God's gifts to me, and they would carry me through the rest of my life. I was a new creation, strong and capable of loving and sustaining my mind, body, and spirit. I no longer needed to be held by the Holy Spirit. My healing transformation was complete. I also understood that I was to share my story with others. Finally, after all these years, I have found the courage to do so.

My story did not end in 2011. My soul's journey has continued through the years to become my never-ending prayer. It is no longer a redemption story but a story of endurance and never-ending love. A love that knows no bounds and is not constrained by time and space. A love so powerful that it will always light the darkness, dispelling any evil in its path. A love that always creates a path of forgiveness and never ceases to flow toward the restoration of peace. A love that never judges but only uplifts those that have fallen, taking them to a place where there is no failure. A love that is given freely from the heart and bound by no conditions. I continue to give and receive this love as best I can, understanding that, in my efforts, I will always find God waiting for me.

I have learned and experienced the power of this love. Indeed, all things are possible when great love is present. I have been totally set free from my addictions. Since 2011, I have experienced great joy in my life but also tremendous waves of stress and sorrow. The challenges that arrived in my life included the deaths of my husband and my father. There were other major shifts as well. Through it all, the grace of God was by my side, and never once did I need or want a drink or a cigarette. I found that when grief, despair, or anxiety appeared, I only needed to meet them with my never-ending love and faith. That was enough to see me through it all. Carrying this love and faith in my heart, I knew I could endure anything.

I am so grateful for all that has been given to me. I am grateful to Mother and Father God, Erob, and Shamoine for their lessons of unconditional love and honor. Most of all, I am grateful to my mother, whose love opened the door to my journey of healing. What she was unable to do for me while living here on earth, she was able to accomplish through the channel of love. Her gift of love was beyond any gift I could have hoped for or dreamed of receiving. There is no greater gift. I am eternally grateful and honored to have received it.

Love never fails.

Love wins.

Always.